Thomas Bartlett Hall, Moses Sperry Beach

Three Articles on Modern Spiritualism

Thomas Bartlett Hall, Moses Sperry Beach

Three Articles on Modern Spiritualism

ISBN/EAN: 9783337427917

Printed in Europe, USA, Canada, Australia, Japan

Cover: Foto ©Lupo / pixelio.de

More available books at **www.hansebooks.com**

THREE ARTICLES

ON

MODERN SPIRITUALISM,

BY

A BIBLE SPIRITUALIST.

BOSTON:

CROSBY AND NICHOLS.

1863.

PRINTED BY FRED ROGERS,
152 WASHINGTON ST.

INTRODUCTION.

THE first two of the Articles published in this little
volume, are reprinted, with slight alterations, from the
"Monthly Religious Magazine" for June and August,
1862. The third Article here added, is substantially a
reproduction of one offered for publication in the same
Magazine, but not then accepted, and the manuscript
subsequently lost.

In willing, but cautious obedience to promptings
which have thus far led him to the beginning, and
successful accomplishment, of many things, often small in
themselves, but serving for an experience to strengthen
his faith, the writer of these Articles has adopted this
more permanent form for their publication; and he now
sends them forth to the world, with an earnest prayer,
that they may accomplish something of the good, for
which alone, he humbly hopes, they have been written.

It seems proper to add, that the Writer has never
been a reader of the leading productions of other pens

upon the topics here treated. He has never read a word in the voluminous works of Swedenborg, or of any of his disciples. Neither has he read any of the writings, with the exception of a few poems, from the pen of the Rev. T. L. Harris, and that school of Spiritualists. His knowledge of Modern Spiritualism is wholly from his own careful, earnest study, and search, into its various phases, in a deep conviction that there must be a mighty truth concealed beneath all the strange phenomena, which would well repay the labor of investigation. He speaks wholly out of his own experience. How far he has been repaid for his patient research, may perhaps be left to the determination of the reader, who is desired to peruse the articles carefully, in earnest seeking for the truth; and especially to discover, and make known, any hidden poison which so many conscientious persons are ready to insist lies concealed in any, the best possible phase, of Modern Spiritualism.

The chief ends sought to be reached in these articles, are :—to show that there is a true spirituality underlying the whole subject ; — to point out briefly the conditions, and explain the difficulties, which have made necessary, the otherwise strange method of its development, out of which all the while is working, in ways as yet little comprehended even by those who have been admitted into its deepest mysteries, the sure fulfilment of things declared in the Scriptures ; — then to show, by brief allusions, the great wants of the modern Christian Church, which cry aloud for something that shall give a new impulse, a new life to its stagnant faith ; — and last, but not least, to declare that Modern Spiritualism has come, not to deny, but to confirm, not to break down, but to strengthen and establish in our minds and hearts, the teachings of the Holy Book, the inspired Word of God, by a new inpouring of the Holy Spirit, amounting, in its fullness, to a new Dispensation.

Thus the three Articles here published seem to complete the preliminary presentation of a subject, which will be exhausted only when Time is lost in Eternity.

BOSTON, January 1, 1863.

Father, I thank Thee! May no thought of mine
Swerve from the path of duty, and of love,
 To Thee, and all mankind.
Help me to know Thee as Thou art,
Give me a loving, true and faith-full heart,
Oh, let me do my humble part,
 In serving Thee!

MODERN SPIRITUALISM.

ARTICLE I.

" The hour cometh, and now is, when the true worshipper shall worship the Father in spirit and in truth."

IT matters not whether we adopt the theory that this globe has, from its infancy to its present state, progressed out of chaos by separate acts of creation, under the fiat of the Almighty; or whether we believe that the process of growth has been one of development out of the life principles so impressed upon the new world at its birth, that time could not go on without their unfolding, gradually, according to a law. The great fact is admitted by all, independently of these theories of growth, that there have been what are conveniently called creative epochs in this world's history, which are distinctly marked as divisions of time, though their precise beginning and ending have eluded the research of the best of our science. There was a time, *we know*, when this earth, now so beau-

1 *

tifully clothed with vegetation, was bare of all growing things. So there must have been, and was, a time
when this vegetation began to creep over the earth's surface. There was a time when there was no animal life
sustained by breathing the earth's atmosphere, and there
was a time when animal life had its beginning. There was
a time, too, when man was not, and a time when he began
to people the earth. These epochs have come gradually,
not only in reference to the whole process of the earth's
development, but, judging from all we can learn by scientific investigation, and from all analogy, each epoch has,
in itself, been the subject of a gradual introduction and
growth, and a gradual decay and disappearance as it has
given way to its succeeding epoch; or rather seems to
have been the foundation on which the epoch succeeding
has been built up. Each new epoch has sprung into
being, not complete and full grown, but from germinal
beginnings that have found their life and sustenance in
the ashes of the past; each successive epoch furnishing,
in its ashes, material for a higher growth in the scale
of being.

These epochs have proceeded in regular series, and the
last so-called act of creation was the coming of man. Of
man's beginning we know nothing. Far back in the
East we discern glimmerings of light upon the questions
when and how the human race begun its career upon
earth; but they are merest glimmerings, and convey to
us nothing more than the beautifully simple record of the
Bible, that God created man in his own image, and he

called their name Adam. Through what vicissitudes of life, what changes and varieties of condition, what growth and refinement, physical and spiritual, this race of beings has been brought to its present development, cannot be stated in any brief compendium. That this world is, however, progressing as heretofore, to some higher condition, and that the beings who are ultimately to inhabit it will rank higher in the scale than its present occupants, is inevitably inferred from all analogy, and is received by all Christians at least, if not by all civilized people, as an event which awaits only the sure fulfilment of prophecy.

No wise man will dare to say that, even in his lifetime, there may not be developments promising things yet to be, which were never dreamed of in his philosophy. We know not when to look for the signs of the coming great change, though we perhaps do know through the Christian dispensation, what the signs shall be, when the great change approaches. That it will be gradual, we argue from analogy, — that it will come silently, without proclamation, "like a thief in the night," we believe from revelation.

It is but a few years since the American public were surprised and amused with the tidings of what was first known as, the "Rochester Knockings." By most persons the story was entirely disbelieved, and deemed unworthy of a second thought, · much less a sober consideration. From that little beginning, what a strange progress and development the thing called Spiritualism, be it true or false, has attained! Subjected to ridicule the most sar-

castic that could be invented; to examinations and tests
of as various kinds as there are variety of conceits
in the human brain; explained, over and over again,
by as many different theories as learned minds to examine,—theories frequently militating against each other,
so that the defender of the cause can often find his best
arguments in the mouths of those who think to condemn;
the most educated classes of the community, with old
Harvard at their head, arrayed in opposition; the Church
issuing its anathemas against it with a bitterness that,
had it been sustained by public opinion, would have
brought the early votaries of Spiritualism to a fiery stake;
little understood, often entirely misunderstood, used and
abused in every conceivable way, still the glaring fact
remains, that no cause, moral or intellectual, civil or
religious, physical or spiritual, ever made such progress in
securing the attention, and the more or less enlightened
faith, of men, than this same cause of Spiritualism. Its
active opponents seem to have pretty much given up their
fruitless attempts to stop it, and to have sunk back from
their labors, seeking consolation in the thought, that, if it
contained no truth, it could not prevail; they have left
it, where indeed they found it, in God's hands, to man-
age according to his own wisdom and high behest. The
result is, as far as our observation goes, that the community is divided upon this subject into two large classes;
namely, those who believe in Spiritualism, in the broad
acceptation of the term, and those who do not believe it,
but think there must, or may be, something in it. The

number of those who utterly reject all its facts and phenomena as trickery, is too small to be named as a class.

Such a subject demands something more than an occasional notice from the pen of journalists, in the ordinary course of comment upon matters that may interest the public. It is, therefore, with no wish to write a passing criticism, or merely to offer a readable article, that we have undertaken to present our views upon Spiritualism; but from an earnest desire to help others to know something of a mighty cause, through the highways and byways of which we have been laboring in the search after truth. Like all pioneers, we have had our experience, which ought to be of value to those who may desire to know the truth like ourselves; and if we can point out any of the dangers, the rocks on which some poor mortal's bark might otherwise be wrecked, we shall feel that we have done some good, whilst we do humbly trust that, as we seek God's blessing on our work, there may be other more positive fruits of our labor. Perhaps what we have to write might be called, the "Confessions of a Medium;" not confessions of our own sins, though God knows we have fallen into errors enough, but confessions of the wonder-workings of an all-wise Father, who rules these things, as all others, — confessions of a deep experience, that has awakened our spirit to new life, and leads it to pray daily that it may be so privileged of God as to do its humble part in bringing his kingdom upon the earth, in seeing to it that his will be done here, even as it is done in heaven. We write what we do know, not what we have heard others tell of. We would be humble as a little child, seeking the truth, with God's blessing on our prayers.

It is about ten years, a little more, since our acquaintance with Spiritualism began through David Hume, of whose medium qualities most persons have heard something. The subject was new then, and people would not believe their senses. Upon his departure for Europe, he was playfully called "Hum-bug." But those who win may laugh; his powers, whatever they were, opened the way for him to the inner chambers of the man who, of all men of this day and generation, has ranked, and still ranks, the shrewdest, sharpest, the veriest juggler, whom nobody would deceive, and whom nobody could find out. This man, the present Emperor of the French, with wit and capacity to detect fraud equalled by few, and with position and power to punish it when detected, without appeal, did not, could not, find the key to Mr. Hume's wonder-workings, except in the explanation which the phenomena have ever claimed for themselves. Before his departure, we had many opportunities of meeting Mr. Hume in private circles and family gatherings, which offered every chance for testing the reality of the phenomena, so that we became fully convinced that they were no ocular delusion, no mistake of our senses, and perhaps might be, what they purported to be, the works of spirit power. It is enough here to say of them, that they combined a variety of physical manifestations, mind-readings, and what purported to be spirit communications, which is not often found in any one medium. He left us wondering; and we looked round for other proofs, other mediums, other experience.

Having advanced so far as to believe in the actuality of the phenomena, doubt not, reader, we soon found ourselves in a very sea of perplexities, and that we were often tempted to give up our inquiry in despair. But remembering that we were pioneers, we determined to brave all hazards, to meet all difficulties, for the sake of truth. Our first great trouble was, that we had ever attached to the word "Spiritualism" a sense of something high and holy; whilst we found neither in the mediums, nor in the phenomena, any special characteristic that marked the high, or the holy; for they partook of all degrees, from the highest of Heaven's blessed truths to the lowest of Hell's horrors. It seemed to us then that the wrong term had been used, and that it should have been Spiritism, or Demonism, in the original sense of demon. And this was, after all, the most natural; for if the good spirits could come to bless us, why could not the bad ones come to plague us; or if the low could come, why not the high? God works by general laws and special providence, in Spiritualism, as in all other things.

Satisfied so far, still we found ourselves continually perplexed, sometimes beyond endurance, by the absurdities, the contradictions, the follies, nay, the wickedness, that broke out upon the community under the guise of Spiritism. With what gratitude did we receive the book published in 1855, by Rev. A. Mahan, President of Cleveland University, entitled, "Modern Mysteries Explained and Exposed." Weary and worn with our labors, ready to sink in the turmoil of doubts that surrounded us, we welcomed that explanation, incomplete though we knew it to be, as sufficient to furnish a retreat wherein we might at least have some rest. He did not pretend to deny the facts of the manifestations, which we knew could not be denied, and so gained our willing concession to his theory of "odilic force." It was sheer fatigue that enabled us to find any rest in this poor shelter; but it sufficed to give us a moment's respite, only to renew the inquiry with increased earnestness, determined, with our own good-will, and in God's own time, to find the truth which we felt assured must be waiting to rejoice those who would strive after it. "Knock and it shall be opened unto you," "Seek and ye shall find," were blessed words of encouragement, which seemed to bring us a new strength. Seeking the truth only for the truth's sake, we trusted that God would guide us, and guard us, through all our deviations from the true path. We prayed to him, that, if there were truth in these things, we too might know, in our own experience, the mysteries of mediumship. We asked that we might know in our own consciousness, through external or internal sense, the actual presence of the spirit world about us. At last the answer began to come. We became sensible of slight touches upon the head, as though a hand were gently passed over it. We had not expected this manifestation, and at first doubted it; but frequent recurrence of the sensation, often under circumstances that caused us much surprise, proved that it was not the work of our imagination, but a real touch from some body or thing, some power or spirit, that thus informed us of its presence, and was perhaps communicating some mysterious influence.

It is unnecessary to describe the stages of development through which we have passed. Suffice it to say, that, though yet far short of the goal, if indeed there be any limit, we have been carried, sometimes quite imperfectly, into enough phases of mediumship to give us an understanding of all these things from our own experience. Each day as we have advanced, the importance of prayer has been urged upon us, and we have felt its power wonderfully in guiding our search for truth, and saving us from the errors committed by others who have not known the wonder working of a true appeal to the Great Father of all spirits. Especially have we been saved from too rapid development, which has so often led men to commit follies that have brought ridicule, and sometimes disgrace, on the very cause they had most at heart. In this, as in all other subjects that may interest and occupy the human mind, too much, or too sudden knowledge, topples the reason, and opens the way for folly to enter in. We have often thanked God in gratitude for the reply made through a medium to our earnest prayer for development: "You shall have the truth as fast as you can bear it; for if it should come as fast as it could be given, it would craze your brain."

We have spoken of passing through certain stages of development *imperfectly*. By this we learned that, whilst such forms of mediumship have their use, particularly for the purpose of introducing Spiritualism to the world's notice, they are not the highest forms. We believe that the highest form of mediumship is that where the individuality of the medium is the most developed and the most active, so that the medium's self, being a spirit in the body, may draw directly from the spiritual fountains of God's eternal truth and power, as mankind has generally believed the spirits of the departed would be privileged to do, according to their spiritual deserving and capacity. In other words, the highest mediumship is what has been heretofore vaguely known as *inspiration*, and sometimes called *genius*. We mean inspiration in its broadest sense, in every kind of knowledge to which the human mind has been permitted to give expression. Religious inspiration, in its various phases; the inspiration of the fine arts, music, poetry, painting, sculpture; the inspiration of the mechanic arts in all the phases of invention; the inspiration of the philosopher; the inspiration of what is often called plain common-sense. They all flow from the same source, — God's great fountains of knowledge. As Solomon said, there is nothing new under the sun. All knowledge exists in spirit life before man slowly elaborates it for external expression on this earth plane, and the degrees of so-called genius are marked by the varying capacity to receive and express it. This idea is involved in the word *impression*, so often used by men in their every-day business affairs. They have "impressions" so and so; sometimes against the convictions of their reason. Where do these impressions come from? What are they? They are the result of influences from spirit life that surround every human being, that "cloud of witnesses," of which we read in Scripture; and they will be of a higher or lower character, exactly according to the spiritual condition of each individual. God works through agents more or less directly. The spirits in the spirit world are the messengers which bear tidings of good, and of so-called evil, to every one according to his desire and capacity to receive. As this desire and capac-. ity to receive depends, under God's blessing, upon each individual will, so each one of us has to work out his own salvation in very truth. But not without aid: the power of prayer is mighty; the Father of spirits will send us such influences as we truly ask for. Ask, and ye shall receive, — even the desired presence of the blessed spirit of Jesus.

This principle of individuality is one of the most important teachings of Spiritualism, though, we admit, nothing in itself new, and offers, at the same time, the simple explanation of one of the serious difficulties in the way of the public acceptation and acknowledgment of the reality of spirit presence and power. It is the first and last objection of the educated classes, that Spiritualism has given to the world so little, if anything, *new* in science, or indeed in any of the ordinary matters that have heretofore occupied the educated mind. It is true that very little has been given to common mundane science, in distinct propositions, through ordinary mediumistic communications, and it is for the reason, now beginning to be understood, that when God permits the spirit world to draw close to the earth life, he does not intend that the spirits out of the form shall assume all the responsibilities, do all the thinking, perform all the labors, bear all the burdens, of those in the form. Such a course, if permitted, would have directly taken away man's accountability; his individuality would be gone; and so experience has taught very many inquirers that they cannot long act with safety in matters of worldly interest under the sole direction of mediumistic communications. The cause of Spiritualism has seemed to suffer, as unbelievers have had opportunity to point the finger of ridicule at the sad and absurd errors committed by Spiritualists, who have been working out this result of their experience, earning this wisdom for their own, and the world's benefit. It is only when the medium's own spirit is developed, so as to receive impressions direct, that he can with safety act them out through his own enlightened mediumistic consciousness; but even then the promptings must ever be brought to the bar of conscience, God within us; whilst the reason must sit in external judgment to determine pure questions of external prudence and policy. We must ever, as St. Paul says, " try the spirits," that we " may prove them."

At the risk of some repetition, we will endeavor to explain more clearly what may perhaps be called the philosophy of mediumship. When the man of so-called genius finds new ideas crowding into his brain, it cannot be said that he makes them. All the result of the scholar's study is to bring the mind into condition to receive the thoughts that are ever waiting for admission, when the mind is ready and able to accept and comprehend them. It is no mere play of fancy, when the poet begins his labor with an invocation to the muses. It is an act of preparation, to lift the poet's spirit into a condition to receive the poesy that is ready to flow in upon him. The most hard-headed philosopher must be in what he would call, the right spirit, or he cannot think (receive thoughts) effectively. A genius, then, and there are as many kinds of genius as subjects to occupy the human mind, is the medium through whom the ideas floating in the spirit world, existing in the spirit life, are given external expression, so as to be more or less comprehended by the minds of others. The man of genius gives expression to the thoughts which are given to him, and commits them to paper. They are printed in a book. This book in turn becomes the medium for the transmission of the ideas to the ordinary reading minds, which, on their part, must be developed to a condition able to receive the ideas, or the words read are hieroglyphics without meaning. The man of genius gets the ideas by inspiration from the world of spirit; the ordinary man of talent must wade through the printed pages, and receive the same ideas by slow induction, word by word. Precisely as the man of genius receives, and gives ex-

pression to the ideas which are given to him, so Spiritualism teaches us, truth is handed down by gradation from
the central fount of eternal knowledge and truth, through
the various conditions of spirits in the spirit world, who
progress and rise from one to another of those "many
mansions," each nearer to the source of direct inspiration.

Now spirit mediums, as commonly recognized, are supposed, by outside observers, to be the mere instruments
used, or purporting to be used *wholly* by *other spirits* for
purposes of manifestation and communication. The fact
is that there are all degrees of mediumship, from this
entire absence of the medium's self, to the complete
inspiration, where the medium's consciousness and individuality are in full action. They are mediums in this
latter case as much as in the former; the difference being
that, in the latter case, the medium's own spirit uses its
own organism to express the inspiration which is given
to it more or less directly, whilst in the former case,
another spirit controls the medium's body, and is itself
the communicator of thoughts, to which it has been
receptive, and now seeks to express. We believe that
those mediums will give to the world the most new
things, and the highest truths, whose individuality is
never lost, and is in the highest state of development.
Of course those forms of mediumship which only afford
tests of spirit presence, resulting in the identification of
friends who have passed on, are desirable, if not indispensable, to satisfy the preliminary inquiries of those
who begin by being either curious, or anxious, to know

whether the world of spirits is really so near this earth
as it professes to be. But these tests are given quite
independently of any consideration of the medium's own
development. Indeed, the most remarkable tests sometimes have come through those of low condition, phy-
sically and spiritually. These tests are given in a great
variety of forms. A very striking form is in the appearance of the names of departed ones, in letters of red on
the arm; a phenomenon which has astounded many
hundreds of persons, as shown in two mediums recently
in Boston. This class of mediums has been, and still is,
essential to the introduction of Spiritualism to man's
notice and comprehension,—it began with table tipping
and rapping, the first rude alphabet of communication,—
it will disappear when it has done its work. Already
many mediums who have been used only for tests are
losing their powers, or falling off into neglect.

Let it not be supposed, however, that the tendency
of Spiritualism is solely to intellectual development and
manifestation. In accordance with the spirit of this age,
it has found its introduction to the world's notice, in a
great degree, through the intellectual faculties and purely
intellectual observations. It could not have been intro-
duced in any other way to a people like the American
nation, which had become so eager in the pursuit of
material prosperity through intellectual development,
that the nation's heart has needed its present fearful
awakening under the hands of an all-wise Providence,
which, in our belief, is but the beginning of a mighty

struggle for dominion between the powers of good and the powers of evil, that is yet to sweep over the face of the whole globe. This consideration leads us to the higher, or what in common acceptation would be deemed, the more spiritual development of Spiritualism, which is now gradually unfolding to the wonder and delight of all its truest advocates.

Whilst it is admitted that an equal development of heart and head are necessary to make the perfect man, we believe that the heart must be first cultivated, or the head cannot receive true wisdom. Without an understanding of the heart, the knowledge of the head is full of errors that lead the spirit to its ruin. This is no new proposition; the philosophy of it is simple. True heart development brings that *peace* of mind which fits it, the mind, for the highest intellectual conceptions, makes it receptive to the highest truths. Yet the nations who boast of their Christian civilization have ignored it, and set up intellectual idols that have received their souls' devotion for six days in every week, and been hardly forgotten in the midst of their would-be sacred observance of the seventh. Wonderful has been the intellectual and material progress of the nations, and particularly of this people, during the past century; but is it not true that spiritual culture and development have been retarded, if not retrograded, in the same degree? Witness the practical results; see, for example, the utter selfishness of the trading, commercial classes. With few exceptions, every man of them is striving, with his

MODERN SPIRITUALISM. 25

whole soul, to find out, *not* how he can help his neighbor, but how he can get ahead of him. Alas, for such Christian followers! We fear the Founder of their religion would hardly recognize his disciples among them. But this is no place for a homily upon the sins of the nations. We should shrink from such a task under any conditions; to catalogue them only would be a fearful undertaking, for their name is legion.

The feeling that true Spiritualism should have something, if not everything, to do with the understanding of the heart; and the fact that it has thus far, to the view of external observers, seemed to have so little to do with it, has been one great cause of the severest opposition it has experienced. For reasons which we shall hereafter endeavor to state, it appears to us to have been necessary, in the present condition of the world's development, that the near approach and communion of the spirit-world should be brought to the knowledge of mankind in the way it has been. Believing, as the Christian world professes to believe, in the second coming of Jesus, how many are there who would be able to recognize him now in our streets in the humble garb of the Nazarene? The difficulties are immense in the introduction of any really new phase in the world's development, arising out of the conditions of head and heart, into which such new development must gradually work its way. We are able now to see the wisdom that directed events, when the infant Jesus was laid in a manger, he "the Prince of Peace," "the Saviour of the world." As time goes on, the wisdom will be recognized which has directed the course of Spiritualism to its present unfolding, itself but the germ of what is yet to be.

We have spoken of our own continuous and unsatisfactory search after true spiritual mediumship, in the first years of our inquiry. We did not feel that we had arrived at the beginning of the truth, until, some two years ago, we made the acquaintance of a medium who had been developed as such after an anxious study of the Bible. This was a young person, born of true New England parentage, in one of the best of New England homes, of large, healthful physique, with fine intellectual powers, a broad head and large understanding, who had been drawn into the cause against external convictions, as well as the wishes of family and friends; but who could find happiness in no other direction, and alone, before God, trusting the inmost dictates of the still small voice, after many struggles, much wrestling with the spirit, had determined to go forward with the work, whatever it might be, so long as it did not militate with the highest sense of right and duty.

This person, called a healing and developing medium, was not under the control of those who purported to be our relatives, or particular friends in the spirit world, but was wholly influenced by a few choice spirits, who announced, through their unconscious trance possession, that their medium had been selected as an instrument of great good to the world. What that good was, we did not at first understand; we had yet to learn it. The communications were addressed wholly to our physical and spiritual condition, and the work of regeneration that was to be done amongst the people. They were not given in tedious homilies, but came in quiet, natural sug-. gestions, warnings, and advice, accompanied at times with a manipulation of the head, which had a strange soothing, yet invigorating power, easily and early recognized. It was indeed a healing power, and imparted a pure vitality, which by a mysterious process gradually reached the spirit within, and we felt that the old heathen maxim of "sound mind in a sound body," had a spiritual meaning beyond its ordinary acceptation. By slow degrees we began to perceive the refined influence that seemed to rain down upon our heads as we sat in silent waiting. Not knowing what to expect, the light of Heaven gradually illumined our heart, and we were ready to acknowledge that we could perceive a spiritual influx, as we sat for development, which seemed to give us, or itself to be, the true riches of which the Scriptures teach, for it brought with it, in very truth, that peace which passeth all understanding. This is no idle fancy of our own, no mere play of the imagination; others have known it as well as we; it is difficult to describe or explain, but when realized by experience, brings with it a sense of reality such as nothing else seems to give. It seems almost the only reality of life.

At intervals the spirits, through this medium, would reason with us, as Paul, of righteousness; but whenever we asked for tests, such as are given through other mediums, they refused, for the reason that it would be a waste of powers which were dedicated to higher uses, as we have above endeavored to explain. We did not, we could not, accept the full meaning of this at once. Tempted in our progress to pursue comparatively idle inquiries, our prayers, and the kind words of the medium, saved us from dallying by the way-side. Purely intellectual investigation seemed to be for a time forbidden. Our business was with the heart alone. To purify that, to become as a little child, to sit at the feet of Jesus, and receive from his hands something of the Christ-spirit with which he was filled, this was our work, this the present object of life. It was (and is) a realization of the patriarch's dream, in which the angels, God's messengers, are eternally ascending and descending, bearing up to the throne the petitions of his creatures, and bringing back the responses of His mighty love,—responses which teach us to throw away selfishness utterly; to live and labor for others; to dispense widely unto all; to give freely, as we have freely received, these treasures of God's love; to so explain these things, and illustrate them in our lives, that they shall show forth His goodness and glory.

These lessons could not be learned till we had given up our conceit of knowledge obtained through purely intellectual culture; and now, humbled as a child before God, but a man amongst men, we feel ready to begin a good work, rejoicing that we find the yoke so easy, the burden so light.

If we are asked, how can these things be known to all, we say to all, high and low, rich and poor, learned and unlettered, gather yourselves in small circles, two or three together, cheerfully, but soberly, reverently, in the name of Jesus, pray for the light you need, and it shall be given to you. Let as nearly as possible the same persons meet at each successive gathering; let the surroundings be fit for such communion. If the circle be in a family,—and where better can it be?—let the place in the house be selected which is freest from contaminating influences. It would be well for the world if there could be a "holy of holies" in every dwelling-house, where the best influences could be poured down upon those in waiting. Let not the father of the family, the man of business, object that it will interfere with his daily avocations; it will rather give him new strength for all his duties. It is not for the Sabbath only, but every day in the week; whilst it teaches still the true value and use of the great day of rest. But chief of all, let not the man of education, of learning, fancy that his time for study cannot be interrupted for these things. Let him rather forget his pride of intellect, and an humble member of the circle, let him ask for that true light which will illumine his soul, and send its quickening rays into the most hidden corners of his deepest researches. It was in the highways that Jesus found his first believers and disciples; — must it be so still?

But be assured, that to follow these things with trifling curiosity is to expose one's self to the penalties of sacrilege. By laws to which we have referred, you will get just what you seek after. Beware lest you bring to the inquiry too careless a heart, or a head too vain of its understanding. Do not, however, think that you can turn away and neglect these things for one motive or another with impunity. Your likes or dislikes cannot change the orderings of Providence. If the near approach of the spirit world be a fact, then it remains a fact whether you like it or not. On the other hand, if it be true that these influences, for good or for evil, are around about, and so near you, it behooves you to understand their powers and mode of action, lest in your wilful ignorance you suffer approaches to which you would not knowingly be subject. In familiar phrase, if you wish to know what company you keep, ever influencing your feelings, your thoughts, your actions, sometimes much more than the friends and companions seen by your body's eye, look closely into your heart, for as that is, so shall your unseen companions be. You cannot escape it. Understand yourself rightly, make yourself what you know you ought to be, and you will learn to thank God for the sweet angel influences that guide and guard you through every hour of your life.

Let not Spiritualism be rejected by outside observers, because they cannot see any good yet accomplished by it. Misunderstood as it has been, much silent good has been done that is not proclaimed aloud to the world. By it many doubting minds have been established in a faith in the future life of the spirit; whilst many more have been relieved of the most depressing fears of the everlasting retribution, the relentless eternity of punishment, by learning that progress is the law of God's universe in the spirit world, as in the earth life; and the blessed consolation of a divine hope has given them new courage to try to attain a higher, better, holier condition, according to their capacity, and not according to the dogmas of their theology. Still more good has been wrought out of Spiritualism, through the very errors of its early converts. Good has come out of the wrongs committed under the name of Spiritualism, by showing the sad inefficiency of the Christian Church of this day. We say it not in unkindness, but in sadness; we say it not of any particular denomination or sect: it is true of all, as out of all have come those unhappy victims of their own weakness, who have, in the name of Spiritualism, thrown off the cloak of religious observances under which they had concealed the rottenness of their hearts from the world's knowledge, if not from their own, and, availing of the assumed authority of false teachers and prophets, have in their actions confessed their little faith. It is a fearful proof of the want of true Christian grace, of vitality in their faith, that so many professors of the religion taught by Jesus, have been so easily led astray. Let them not make recantations, and lay the blame on Spiritualism, for it is but their own sins which have found them out; they may rather thank God that anything has come to show them their spiritual condition.

Angels are about us, the spirit world has, in this nine-teenth century, been brought near to the earth life to mingle its influences for good, or for evil. Not, as it would seem, by an entirely new law; for these things have been before; but to an extent, and in a manner, which indicate, and are proclaimed as showing, a new dispensation in the providence of God. Exactly what this new dispensation will unfold is not for man to know yet, but that it is ushering in one of those great epochs in the progressive history of the earth and its creatures, to which we have in the beginning referred, we do believe. Far be it from us to presume to reach too far into the plans of the Almighty; but it is our solemn conviction, that these things do announce that *second coming* of which the Scriptures teach. The condition of the earth and its people, the signs of the times, indicate this more than ever before; whilst the near presence of the spirit world brings with it holy influences which must elevate and spiritualize all of earth's creatures who will receive them, and, as good is ever stronger than evil, will, sooner or later, drive off into outer darkness all who wilfully reject and oppose them out of the ignorance, or the wickedness, of their hearts. *If God's holy angels can and do so come, why may not the blessed spirit of Jesus come too? Has he not come already? Is he not in the midst of us even now, and we know him not?*

MAY, 1862.

ARTICLE II.

" Behold, I make all things new."

HAVING endeavored to show that there is a true spirituality underlying the external expression of Modern Spiritualism, we would now try to remove the chief obstacle which has prevented many conscientious persons from finding out this inner life, by explaining the origin, growth, and present state of the antagonism between intellectual, and pure spiritual culture. This branch of the inquiry may not be interesting to all readers, but we deem it indispensable that it should be thoroughly examined, and fully comprehended, before the more educated part of the community, as a whole, can be in condition to receive the truth. We would reiterate, that we write wholly from a desire, under God's blessing, to give to others the light which has been given to us; understanding that what we have to say cannot of itself persuade, but only make others receptive to the *influences* which God is ready to pour in upon all who will open themselves to the *"flowing in of his spirit of love and truth."*

Nothing is more marked in the history of opinion, whether relating to the commonest interests of every-day life, or to the most abstruse problems of scientific or

2 *

metaphysical inquiry, than the disposition of mankind to incline to extremes; on the one side in their tenacity of things already established, and on the other side in their correction of acknowledged errors. Discovering their mistakes slowly, men are apt to adopt views directly opposite to the old ones, and for that reason full of new error. Whether this arises from a laudable desire to find the truth, and hold it firmly when discovered, or whether it has its origin in man's weak conceit, leading him to assume the right and power to fix the limits of knowledge, and declare out of his own mouth the law, to the conception of which he has slowly attained, is a question which we believe might be carefully considered with much profit to self-sufficient humanity. The fact is admitted by all; and the leaders in these opposite positions are deemed the extremists of their time, and properly so considered, whether they are on the side of progress or conservatism. Few, however, are able, though recognizing the fact, to attain a position nearer to the truth; whilst most are content to flatter themselves by pointing out the extreme views of others, and pronouncing judgment on them even to foolishness.

Of all extremists none are so unhappily placed, at least for their own advantage, as those who are on the side of conservatism; their case is almost hopeless. The extremists of reform are ever moving on to new thoughts and new life; making mistakes enough in their self-anointed conceit, but still getting lessons in their experience which their conceit would not let them learn by

the gentler processes prepared by God for the teaching
of those his children who are willing to humble themselves first before him, in prayer for such light as he will
vouchsafe to give them in his own time, and in his own
way. Alas for the extremists of conservatism! They
never try to rise; they wish for nothing new, no matter
how much for the better. They remain, as they suppose,
firmly fixed on everlasting truth; till suddenly they discover that the foundation on which they rested has
rotted away, or become too weak for the superstructure;
and from being the most comfortably secure, they find
themselves the most uncomfortably insecure of all the
world. Inevitably they either float off without sails,
without rudder, without compass, into a turbulent sea of
doubt and distraction; or, as the old ties give way, they
swing violently to the other and directly opposite extreme, yielding themselves to a mixed rule made up
largely of temper and selfish chagrin, though its true
character may be concealed from themselves by their
declared and acknowledged desire to do as nearly right
as they can. Their motive may seem to be good; but
they were extremists in their conservatism, and they
are become extremists in their new light. We have
remarkable instances of this in the political relations of
the American people at the present time, when the most
ultra conservatists give expression to violent sentiments
which fairly leave behind many of those whom they
formerly decried as dangerous, if not unprincipled reform-
ers. The same thing may be seen in all the relations

of life, if we will observe them carefully, even in the most insignificant matters.

It is not to be expected that men should be otherwise affected, and experience shows that they are not, in matters regarding their religious and spiritual interests. A few centuries ago, the civilized world was wholly subjugated to the Church, which had usurped to itself all authority over the minds and hearts of men, so that both in mind and heart man's individuality was lost. In knowledge of temporal things he became a child; and whenever the spirit world and its influences came near him, he fell at once into blind superstition, which culminated, at different intervals among the nations, in the various phases and terrors of witchcraft.

This assumption of the Church, arrogating to itself all knowledge, all power, in things temporal, and in things spiritual, though under the name of spiritual rule only, led to the Reformation of the seventeenth century. Breaking from the thraldom in which he had been held, man rushed into the arena which he found world-wide,— nay, limited only by the limits of his own capacity. Not all at once did he obtain freedom from church rule. Even now it is far from complete in things purely spiritual; for the dogmatic theology of Protestantism has at times held, and does in some directions now, well-nigh hold, in spiritual things, the very supremacy which led to the outbreak of the seventeenth century. But the old impulse, the return pendulum-swing of opinion started by the Reformation, continues; and, believing that the old error was, in yielding a blind obedience to the rule of those who pretended to act wholly under spiritual guidance, and thus made distrustful of all things purely spiritual and cognizable first, if not wholly, by the heart, man still is, as he has been, for the last two or three centuries, going to the other extreme, and letting intellectual forces take the lead and control of his development. The result is a disposition to doubt everything not the subject of absolute independent intellectual conception, and this has led, in different nations and at different periods, to conditions fatal to his highest spiritual development. In France, it reached a climax in the fearful reign of Reason, and the bloody scenes of her great Revolution. Throughout all Europe it has resulted often in a miserably unspiritual, if not wholly Godless materialism. In our own country the tendency has been to a materialism, not Godless, but wholly unspiritual. The intellectual conception of the God principle has been retained, and he has been permitted to reign abstractly through such laws as science has been able to investigate; but he has been a God of the head only, not of the heart. The tendency has been to recognize his power in the world's creation, and perhaps in the daily orderings of the world's life, but to ignore and deny the possibility of a spiritual relation between man and his Creator, other than man's ever-varying conceptions of his attributes.

In struggling to escape from the thraldom of the old church, man has succeeded so far as to be no longer subject in temporal things, and to a great extent in spiritual

things, to its dominion. We see comparatively little of
the old superstitious relation between the priest and the
people. But in denying the authority of the Church,
and exercising his own thought upon spiritual things,
man has been carried to the opposite extreme of independence, and come to rely wholly on his own strength,
forgetting that there was a God behind the Church,
whose power, whose love, the Church had arrogated to
itself, and therefore lost its influence. Nay, the individual man has fallen into the very error which has led
to the destruction of the Church's power, and consti-
tuted himself as the Church, with all knowledge, all
power. As surely as the Church has lost its high position and power, so surely must individual man be humbled before the true, the only Church, which is of Christ.
"It may or may not be a matter of regret," said an ob-
servant preacher, recently, "that church organizations
seem to be crumbling; the great fact is left, that, where
two or three are gathered together in the true Christ
spirit, there will always be a true Church." He might
have added, there only has the true Church ever been.

Still, progress is the law; and from this extreme intellectual development has come the power to resist the
tendency to superstition in spiritual things which was
almost unavoidable during man's thraldom to the Church,
—a power without which he would not have been able
to bear the recent advent of spiritual phenomena. The
want of this power is even now shown in many individuals, who from mere fear are unable to approach the sub-

ject of Spiritualism, as presented in the more striking physical manifestations, though few are bold and truthful enough to themselves and their fellows to acknowledge their weakness. The old church superstition is not all . worked out of them, though they little suspected it till these recent strange things forced them to show the fact in their actions, if not in words. A few of these timid ones try to persuade themselves that their fear is a proper fear of trenching upon sacred ground, an unwillingness to pry into the things upon which God has set the seal of mystery. But these either deceive themselves as to the fact, or their feeling is but another form of the old superstition which taught that the priest alone could know the ways of God. Let them remember that Christ died for all men, and to all men is it given to penetrate the very depths of spiritual things, if they will become worthy to be so blessed. To him that asketh, if it be in the right spirit, it shall be given. To him that knocketh in the name of Jesus, it shall be opened.

Believing, then, that out of this intellectual freedom has come to most men of this day and generation the ability to bear the approach of spirit phenomena, so far as to examine them without falling into the old superstition of witchcraft, we would endeavor to show more particularly how this has been brought about; to explain the working of the elements of head and heart, mind and spirit, which have heretofore held such antagonistic relations, and thus to reach, if we can, the true philosophy of this branch of the subject. We ask the candid reader's careful attention.

Thought and spirit are real things. They have substance, refined, as compared with material things, even up to sublimity; still they are real, substantial existences. It is difficult for us to come to a conception of this idea, this fact; and perhaps it is sufficient for the present to recognize them only as forces, of substance too ethereal and sublimated to be cognizable by the senses of the body, yet living forces. Now it cannot be denied that, since the Reformation of the seventeenth century, it has been the ever-increasing tendency of Protestantism to give unlimited sway and supremacy to intellect, and to reject all phenomena, all manifestations, which could not be discerned through the ordinary avenues of intellectual conception, and recognized through the ordinary channels of external sense. Thus, by the deliberate exercise of his will, the forces of man's intellect have been held in direct and successful opposition to the forces of his inner or spiritual life. The idea of spiritual discernment, as understood in the days of the Apostles, has been utterly repudiated, as having no possible place in our wise-thinking heads, and any suggestion of such a possibility in these days utterly rejected. Here is a plain, direct antagonism between subjects of external intellectual conception, and things of the spirit, to be spiritually discerned. From this antagonism has arisen the difficulty, especially of educated people, in receiving

spirit manifestations, whether of the purer and more refined, or of the grosser kinds; there being as many
degrees of refinement among spirits, as mansions to
receive them in the spirit world. The more men have ·
been educated in the schools of the day, the greater has
been their difficulty as regards these spiritual things.
Too great confidence in their intellectual acquirements,
or, to speak in plain terms, though not in unkindness,
their self-reliant intellectual conceit, has repelled, or
made impossible, all direct approaches from the spirit
world. Herein we find the key to what has heretofore
been considered the mystery of faith. There are three
conditions to which the idea of faith has relation. First,
entire disbelief; second, indifference as to belief, or mere
willingness not to reject; and, third, active belief. In
these three conditions are the three degrees: first, direct
antagonism of the intellectual forces against the spiritual
forces; second, a mere suspension of hostilities, with
more or less of a guard to watch the enemy; and, third,
the open receptiveness, the glad welcome to all the gifts
and graces of the spirit, with all their accompanying
blessings as they are worked out into external, or more
material expression, on the earth plane.

There is no new law in these conditions. It prevailed
equally in those early days when the Holy Spirit was
manifested on earth in the form of Jesus. It was
amongst the ignorant fishermen that he, the Nazarene,
the carpenter's son, found his first disciples; simple-
minded men, who had nothing to unlearn, and little, if

any, intellectual antagonism to overcome. The educated men of his day would not receive him. To the fishermen it was enough for him to say, " Follow me,"—whilst it required a miraculous intervention to reach the heart of Paul. So, too, in the more external workings and expression of the spirit power, what might be called the more physical manifestations of spirit, wrought out through Jesus, the same law prevailed; and we are told in the Scripture record, that the want of faith, or rather their active disbelief, the intellectual antagonism, prevented a certain district of the Jewish people from beholding the wonder-workings of the miraculous power. Οὐκ ἠδύνατο ἐκεῖ οὐδεμίαν δύναμιν ποιῆσαι, εἰ μὴ, &c., " And he could there do no mighty work, save," &c.; *was not able to do* is the literal translation, as it is the only meaning of the original Greek, though commentators find great difficulty in accepting it, because of the standpoint from which they take their view.*

By this same law of antagonism between mind and spirit power, have many persons been utterly prevented from witnessing even the grossest forms of spirit manifestation in these latter days. Learned men, relying on the education of their heads, have again and again endeavored to hear even the simple rappings, with more or less conscious desire and will, not to find out what the strange thing was, but to prove that it was not what it

---

* Gospel according to Mark, chap. vi. verses 5 and 6; also Matthew, chap. xiii. verse 58. See note to this last verse in Barnes's Notes on the Gospels.

purported to be; and they have gone away reassured in their wisdom of this earth, which in such an inquiry is indeed very "foolishness."

In obedience to this same law, there was a gradual dis-. appearance, and latterly, up to the commencement of the rappings, there has been a remarkable cessation of all the manifestations, which in the days of church rule resulted in superstition and witchcraft. Appearing at intervals in the gradual decline of the Church's power, the fact of this final entire cessation has always been to our minds, until recently, quite inexplicable. Here and there, to be sure, we had heard of what were called haunted houses, and we had read of the Wesley rappings; but our education had taught us to consider all such things as manifestations of anything but spirit power, and most probably as the result of deluded imaginations. Still, Mansfield on the English bench, and Sewall on this side, had soberly sat in judgment, and had condemned on the evidence; and the alternative has been either to deny the facts and stultify Mansfield and Sewall, as indeed we believe Sewall, later in life, did for himself; or to admit the facts in some way, and wonder why such things had so entirely disappeared in modern times. We now understand that this cessation of spirit manifestations has been owing to the power of mental forces, held by the will in antagonism with the spirit forces.

Let it be supposed, then, for the sake of the argument, if the position cannot otherwise be admitted by our readers, that, in the fullness of time, the period had come when the spirit world was moved through its depths to draw near to the earth life. How could it, under the condition of things which we have endeavored to explain, how could it signify its approach and near presence? It has often been objected to modern spirit phenomena, that their method of expression is so mundane, so unspiritual, though claiming to be of spirit origin. The objectors have demanded that the spirits should come with gentler approaches, and in more ethereal guise. But it must be remembered that spiritual things, in what may be termed their more natural expression, can only be spiritually discerned; and how, we would ask, could these spiritual things be discerned by a race who utterly repudiated the possibility of such a manifestation, and deemed such an idea foolishness? Nay, how could the spiritual world even come near enough to be spiritually discerned by a people who were all the time repelling it, by the antagonism of which we have spoken? A little reflection shows that it was only through material signs, to be recognized by the senses of the material body, that the spirit world could begin to effect any approach. It was because the world in the flesh was deaf to the still small voice, that resort to the gross, or material manifestations, by rappings, was necessary. Even these manifestations owed part of their influence to, if they were not necessarily preceded by, the phenomena of mesmerism or animal magnetism, to the laws of which recourse has so often been had for an explanation of the spirit phenomena, which otherwise would have compelled many minds to

admit that they were what they purported to be. Thus
gradually, through the three degrees above named as
associated with the idea of faith, has the antagonism been
removed, and thus is it still being removed, and the opposition so disarmed, that the finer, and purely spiritual
manifestations begin to be received by those who have
clambered over the stumbling-blocks in their way, and to
the spiritually-developed the things of the spirit begin to
be opened, and by them spiritually discerned. But, oh!
through what struggles, what sufferings has this knowledge of spiritual things been attained. The utter re-
pudiation of the possibility of spirit expression and communion has led to public and private persecution worthy
of other days. Men have charged the folly, if not the
crime, of superstition upon all the early votaries of modern Spiritualism; and public opinion, instead of the burn-
ing stake, has been, and still is, the fiery ordeal to which
the conscientious believer finds himself bound in bitter
agony, whilst nearest and dearest friends are willing to
add fuel to the fire, and blow the flame, till the victim
yields his faith, or through spiritual power is raised tri-
umphantly, like the martyrs of old, above all consciousness of suffering.

By degrees the supremacy of pure intellectual knowledge and insight is giving way; and, having become
willing to throw aside their conceit of intellect, men are
beginning to sit down humbly before true spiritual culture, and receive the inspirations from spirit life that have
long been waiting to bless them, but they would not

accept. Their intellectual development has liberated men from those idle fears and low conceptions which formerly led to witchcraft and its fearful persecutions; whilst the same condition of development has led, at the outset of the investigation of modern Spiritualism, to purely intellectual conceptions of the subject, through inquiries originating in the head, much oftener than in the heart. The idle curiosity, flattering itself often under the guise of scientific authority, which has from the beginning put the questions suggested by its vain conceit, has been met and answered in a way well calculated to put it to the blush. The spirit of the inquiry has been promptly met by its brother spirit in the spirit life; and all by the force of laws which the wise in the wisdom of this earth have been slow to comprehend, assuming that they were already well enough informed on all matters of spirit life, power, and manifestation, because they had reached to a comprehension of some of the laws by which its Creator regulates his material creation.

It may be claimed by different branches of the Christian Church, that they do not deny the proper supremacy of pure heart culture when brought into comparison with the wisdom of the head, though they perhaps have not distinctly recognized the antagonism which we have shown to exist. In the Catholic Church, particularly, has the position been maintained, and practically carried out, that the danger in giving free scope to intellectual investigation in spiritual things certainly, and perhaps to some extent in temporal things, was so great, that the

popular mind could not bear exposure to it, and hence
the argument in support of blind church rule, and mysterious rites in their religious services, conducted in an
unknown tongue by the initiated priest. So, too, with ˉ
the dogmas of the Protestant churches, insisted upon as
articles of faith, and involving points of doctrine which
had been worked out by the leaders of the Church, who
alone could be lifted up to a true contemplation of their
inner sense ; a position of strange inconsistency for Protestantism, as recognized by all freethinkers, and justly
rebuked by the parent church. But, passing by this
question of inconsistency, and admitting the merit in this
fear of intellectual supremacy, let us look a little at the
character of the substitute offered in compensation for
the loss of the intellectual investigation which has not
been permitted. It is in this direction, and it seems to us,
that the Church has deceived itself, and out of this self-
deception that it is so powerless to put an end to the
fearful sway of selfishness, which now rules with nations
and individuals. So much stress has been laid upon the
importance of articles of faith, that the masses have been
content with holding to these, if indeed they have not
been directly taught that these alone were sufficient for
their salvation. Catholicism and dogmatic Protestantism
have pointed out a danger in too independent action of
the intellect upon spiritual things, but their position in
this regard has been substantially a negative one only, so
long as they have furnished no better substitute for the
right of free inquiry than simple obedience to their own

authority, whether expressed in blind church rule, or
theological dogmas. Thus has it happened that all the
while, in spite of Catholic church rule and Protestant
dogmatic authority, the intellectual forces of men, starved
into independent self-reliant action, have been attaining
the ascendency each day more and more, and the antagonism of which we have spoken become established.

If the Church had not assumed to possess all knowledge
and all power in spiritual things, and taken upon itself
the responsibility of true enlightenment, thus relieving
men of their individual responsibility to know and understand their true relation to God and their fellow-men; if
it had not offered itself as the Mediator between them
and their Creator, but had rather denied itself alway,
and offered Christ as the only Mediator; if by its own
example it had taught men to humble themselves, each
one, before God, in prayer for such light and such blessings as he might see were needed, and vouchsafe to send
them; then indeed would a good work have been done, and
the Church of this day been entitled to a tribute of praise
and thanks from its equally humble followers. But pride,
conceit, and self-reliance have been its attributes, and its
children could hardly be expected to be superior to their
spiritual guide. The happy middle course of humble,
prayerful, individual development was hard to find out
under such conditions; and few, very few, have found
and followed it.

We do not understand, and would not for a moment
suggest, that the intellectual faculties of our nature are

to be lost, or even kept in abeyance, but made subordinate to pure heart or spiritual culture, so that only true knowledge can, and shall, be offered to man's comprehension. Then all things of the spirit shall be accepted by, and made reasonable to, the mental faculties, which will sit humbly waiting for God's movement, and not trusting in themselves to work out their own knowledge in their own way, which leadeth to destruction. The equal development of heart and head, the beautiful harmonious result of a true relation between the spiritual and mental forces, in which alone can be found the perfect man, is yet to come; and the grave question now proposed to the world is, whether the time for the establishment of that harmonious relation is not at hand! It can come in no other way than through a pure spiritual Christianity, such as the world has not seen yet, with the Christ spirit, and not human intellect, under any guise of creed or doctrine, recognized as the only test of a true church. It is then, and not till then, that the prayer so often on the lips of men is to be answered; then, when God's kingdom shall come, and his will be done on earth, even as it is done in heaven.

If it be true — and Spiritualists know it to be true — that messages from angel forerunners have announced the coming of that kingdom as close at hand, when Christ shall return to earth, and reign in the name of the Father, is it well, nay, is it safe, to pass the messengers, or the message, by unheeded? If it should be that they are messengers of truth, are you ready, are you prepared, to

3

bear the *quickening power* of the Spirit? Already is it
at the nation's door. Already have the elements of war
and fratricidal strife in this people been worked out into
fearful expression. Be not deceived because this appears
to have been done by natural causes. Wait not till the
influence has penetrated to the very hearthstones of your
homes, for there too shall its quickening power yet be
felt, and the elements of disease and death be driven out
into expression more fearful even than on the battle-field.
Purify your homes, purify your hearts, purify your bodies,
purify your lives! Wait not for the purification which
shall be a consuming fire. Even now does the mighty
voice sound through the air, as heard of old by the
Prophet of Revelations, and audible to him that hath an
ear to hear are those momentous words, "BEHOLD, I
MAKE ALL THINGS NEW!"

JULY, 1862.

ARTICLE III.

" And he shewed me a pure river of water of life."

AGAIN we find ourselves filled to overflowing with thoughts restlessly demanding expression. Again we are moved by a deep heart-felt desire to communicate to others, would it could be to all the world, some idea of the rich blessing, the joy unspeakable, which we have received from a knowledge of things spiritual, as opened to us through Modern Spiritualism. We say *knowledge* of things spiritual: for it is no conventional creed; no philosophical, or mystical, shaping of our human conceit; no ingenuity of our poor brains. It is knowledge in very truth: a certainty; an experience; a living reality; without which now, life would become to us almost insupportable, the world would seem a barren waste deprived of the indispensable sunlight of God's love. The soul recognizes and rejoices over this blessing, the richest in the Father's bestowal, at all times, and in all events. It is drawn in with every breath; it courses through every vein; it moves, it leads, it guides, it guards, in every emotion, every thought, every action of our waking, or sleeping existence. It is the presence of the living God! The willing spirit listens to its heart promptings, and child like yields every wish of its own to the gentle ruling

of a Father's love. Under its influence, human pride
is let down from all assumption and conceit. The soul
recognizes in its inner sense, and its outer experience,
that the divine guidance is ever directing and helping in
matters seemingly the most trivial, as well as in those
otherwise supposed to be most momentous, and so goes
on in its daily occupation, rejoicing equally in large and
small duties, for in all and each, it humbly feels that it
is doing, or at least trying to do, only the Father's
will.

As we look into the world of life around us, we feel,
we know, that there too, as well as in ourselves, the
power of God, is alive and at work; and no living
creature, no created thing, is too insignificant to be a
sharer of our sympathy as coming from the hand of the
same maker with ourselves, and sustained by the same
love. Thus no difference of external position, or surroundings; no apparent preference or exhaltation of one
creature above another, of one human being over his fellows astonishes or deludes us into anything like creature
worship, or brings any the least desire to sacrifice to
worldly pomp or circumstance. All creatures and all
things are in their proper sphere and place, moving on
in accordance with a mighty law of development, which
no man can fully comprehend. Happy those who can
recognize the Father's guiding and sustaining hand
through it all. Thrice happy those who can fall gently
in with the current, and acquiescing in the wisdom of all
things, without struggle or resistance, humbly seek the

more to know and feel the Father's ever present protection and care, the more the course of events, near and far, large and small, becomes complicated and inexplicable to their feeble comprehension. Oh, that this faith, . this living faith could be a reality of experience to all. May God's blessing go with our humble effort to communicate and explain to others something of this life, divine, so that the desire in their hearts may unfold into a faith that shall open them to the influences of the Holy Spirit. Thou knowest, Father, that this wish is expressed in no vain conceit of our own wealth; that it is no foolish boast of the blessings with which Thou hast crowned our life. As we are true unto the truth as it is in Christ, be Thou unto us, and unto this labor!

"That the desire in their hearts may unfold into a faith that shall open them to the influences of the Holy Spirit"! Let no one take offence at this; but rather let every one inquire soberly what it signifies. What does it mean, that in this day of Christian development, with so many men and women to be found throughout this religiously enlightened people, who have experienced the movings of the spirit within, and become, in the church sense, reconciled unto God, and with so many more who have felt their inner natures touched by the divine presence, and the secret chambers of their hearts illumined by a divine light, not their own; what does this call mean, which says to such, and we gladly admit there are many such, that their faith needs yet to be unfolded, and their hearts to be "opened to the influences of the

Holy Spirit"? Certainly it is not intended to be a
captious, fault-finding complaint, or rebuke. It is rather
an invitation to still further development, to a finer
growth, a higher life of the spirit, a more complete realization, in every day practical life, of all the blessings
which are involved in, and spring from, the Christian
faith; a more abundant blossoming and fruition in those
gifts and graces of the spirit, which in the days of the
early disciples of Jesus were distinctly recognized as the
natural outgrowth, as they were the visible evidences of
a true Christian life. The highest received Christianity
of the churches of to-day, stops far short in its practical
outworking of the Christianity taught, and if we may
believe the record, actually realized amongst the early
converts, the first disciples of the humble Nazarene. And
this without any reason, or explanation, offered or received; and when referred to by some honest enquirer
for a cause, is admitted, with the cold, insufficient comment, that those times are not these times. In other
words, the men and women of those days, when the
world was almost two thousand years younger in its
development than now, are admitted to have been capable of spiritual attainments, which we of this day cannot aspire to! What has the world been about all this
time, that such should be the comparative condition of
those who are so apt, in all other things, to boast of their
modern civilization! Can it be believed, that the good
seed sown by the Master's hand has been all this time
germinating, the divine influence by him implanted

upon our earth sphere has been so long, and so widely, rooting, without some progress in the capacity of man's nature to receive, and express, a higher type of Christian development, than it was possible for the men of the early centuries to attain; instead of our being unable even to equal them! The truth is, not only that the good seed has been germinating, but that the natural man has been going through a process of decay. There has been a breaking down of the walls of the flesh; human nature has been changing; becoming less and less gross in its animal development, and consequently more and more susceptible to spirit influences; and that the manifestations of spirit presence and power in these days, are uncontrovertible evidences of the fact. But we may be content, for the present, to rise to those spiritual attainments with which, the record tells us, the early Christian disciples were blessed. When those are reached, it will be time enough to aim at higher growth, and loftier elevations, of the spirit's life.

The first step towards progress is the admission of present wants, the acknowledgment of present short comings, the recognition of something better and higher, which we have not yet reached. Every one admits that there is no condition so fatal to Christian development, as a satisfaction and contentment with present attainments. In order therefore that the class of professing Christians, to whom we have above referred, may be reminded how far short they are of the living faith which Jesus offered to his contemporaries, and by the wonder-

fully preserved record, as well as by the influences now
pouring in upon the world, offers unto us, we would ask
such to put a few searching questions to themselves,
which shall reach to the heart, without disguise of any
sort.   When those questions have been seriously considered, they will be more willing to admit the necessity,
and better able to receive the blessings, of a new dispensation, whose first work is to revivify the ancient faith
which bears such stinted fruit in their lives.

Beginning with the more visible signs of faith ; where
do we find a professor of the Christian life in these days
who, through his religious development, can show, we do
not say boast of, for they are in no sense a subject for
pride, any of those signs, which in the words of Jesus,
as recorded by St. Mark, "shall follow them that believe"—"In my name," said the Master, "shall they cast
out devils; they shall speak with new tongues; they
shall take up serpents; and if they drink any deadly
thing, it shall not hurt them; they shall lay hands on
the sick, and they shall recover"! Who of them, we
ask, can show a faith responsive to those other words
recorded by St. John, "He that believeth on me, the
works that I do, shall he do also, and greater works
than these shall he do"! Who, again we ask, can show
any of those gifts of the spirit enumerated by St. Paul
as the natural result and evidence of a knowledge of
Christ, when accompanied with the gift of charity?
How is it that none of these persons can show even the
signs and gifts which have, in these latter days, made

their appearance amongst so many that are not recognized as the truest followers of Christ, if indeed they are not often wholly without that spirit of charity, or love, the want of which, says St. Paul so truly, renders these gifts valueless. It may almost be said, that instead of the members of the modern Christian church showing in themselves any of the gifts of the spirit, they are apt to condemn unheard any one who seems to possess these gifts, as on that very account, to be excluded from the Christian fold!

But passing by these external evidences recognized by Christ himself as signs of those who believe in him, what are the inner proofs of progress in true Christian development to be found in the professing members of the modern church? For example, how many of these have comprehended the meaning, and practical application, of the Saviour's reference to the lily of the field, as a beautiful examplar for man to copy in his daily life? How many are there who begin to take no thought for the morrow, what they shall eat, or what they shall drink, or wherewithal they shall be clothed? How many who really believe, and carry into practice their faith, that if they will seek the Kingdom of Heaven first, all those things "shall be added unto them." To earn a livelihood, to gain an independence, is proclaimed and approved as the great aim, the first object of every man's ambition; not to find out what service his Creator would have him do, what field is open for him to accomplish the highest, greatest good; not what the unselfish promptings of the

3 *

spirit within would have him attain to, but what avenue
is most open by which he can reach what his friends,
and all the world, call success. Occasionally, to be sure,
a young man begins his career with vague notions of
usefulness; but they are either soon crushed out of him
by contact with the stern realities of life, which come to try
him, and prevail against his better feelings, for the reason
that he has not that living faith which can sense and
follow, the leadings of the Spirit, and patiently leave
results to the wisdom of God; or he sinks in despair at
the apparent fruitlessness of his efforts, and dies early of
a broken heart. The pulpit does indeed insist upon the
absolute importance of every man's loving God with his
whole heart, being just in all his dealings, and in short
carrying his religion into his business; but does it suffi-
ciently teach that a true development in Christ is itself
a business, the first business, it may almost be said, the
only business that peremptorily demands his attention;
for the Kingdom of Heaven first attained, the fruits of
all other business shall, in natural course, be added unto,
and crown his life with many joys. Men and women
have yet to feel that in the performance of all the daily
avocations of life, in every position and capacity, they
are doing God's business, not their own! When they
can feel this, the work of life, in all its details, will go
on with a harmony that shall chord with the very music
of the spheres; for then will they have sought the kingdom of Heaven first, and will do their daily labor, not
for the sake of the bread that shall be earned by it, but for

the joy in doing the Father's will; trusting that their daily bread will be given to them in due season in answer to their daily prayer, as naturally, and as surely, as the elements bring to the lily of the field the food it needs· for its daily growth, and the materials wherewith to weave the beautiful fabric of its matchless raiment.

A much severer test of the development of those who openly and formally profess their faith in Christ, is to be found in their conduct at this period of national judgment and condemnation, when if ever there seems to be a call for all the cardinal Christian virtues, FAITH, HOPE and CHARITY. We feel that the leading spirit of the great Southern Rebellion is a wicked one. We believe equally, that many, if not the most of the combatants on both sides, certainly of those who have gone forth to crush it with death-bearing weapons of war, have been, and are, actuated by their highest sense of self-sacrificing duty, and shall receive their reward accordingly. But do these considerations alter the fact that war is not, and cannot by any sophistry be made, consistent with the teachings of the gentle Jesus, whom they in other things profess to follow. Undoubtedly every man does right who acts up to his highest sense of duty ; but is that sense of duty necessarily according to the Christ-spirit of love, because it is the man's highest sense ? The highest sense of duty with the ancient Jew was in exact retaliation, " an eye for an eye, a tooth for a tooth." But Christ has taught, nay, in love commanded, " That ye resist not evil : but whosoever shall smite thee on thy

right cheek, turn to him the other also." " Love your
enemies, bless them that curse you, do good to them
that hate you, and pray for them which despitefully use
you and persecute you" are the words of the Master,
spoken without reservation of any kind. Some persons,
a little more tender than others, feeling the inconsistency,
have talked about laying aside their Christianity for the war,
as they, with their short external vision, have found themselves unable to see how the struggles of the day could be
carried out to a successful issue without the recourse to
arms ; instead of acting up to their inner sense of Christian
duty, and leaving results to Him who rejoices more to be
worshipped as a God of love and peace, than appealed
to as a God of Battles. Have these persons forgotten
how the walls of Jericho fell down at the sound of
trumpets blown with a blast of *living faith !* Have they
never read how, more than once, the enemies of Israel
were scattered by the interposition of divine power,
without a blow struck by the Sword of Gideon ; and this
long before the people were blessed with the light of the
Gospels ! Is it not time the world began to understand,
that if in the orderings of God's providence there is need
of men to fight, it is because there are men whose
progress in Christian development has not yet rooted
out the elements of war from their natures. No pure
health can be enjoyed by the human system so long as
disease is lurking in the vital parts ; and as long as the
passions that culminate in war are circulating in humanity, no matter how deep under the surface, so long

will occasions be presented for working them out; it being always the prerogative of God, and of Him only, to bring good out of this direful evil.

If we are asked what we would have men do in this emergency of the nation's existence, we would say, let every one go to his God in humble, earnest prayer for such knowledge as shall show him his highest duty, and when found, do it unselfishly, with all his might. Let him not however deceive himself by supposing that he is therefore acting up to the Christ teachings, because he is fulfilling what he finds to be his highest duty. But let him rather pray the more earnestly to God that he may receive the true Christ spirit, and sense of Christian duty, the more he finds himself called to acts at variance with the clear, unmistakable precepts of the Founder of his professed faith; for *it is a thing of growth*, and nothing short of miraculous intervention will give him the true sense, the true light at once. The trouble is, that men, having no knowledge of, and giving no recognition to the guidance of the Spirit, use their minds first to find out what course of conduct to pursue, and then go to God to ask his help in carrying out *their* plans of management; instead of lifting up their hearts first in humble prayer to Him for guidance, and then following the lead of the Spirit with all their minds! Thus it is that we have had all the while the strange spectacle presented, apparently so contradictory, in the civil war now raging, of clergy and laity on both sides, sending up fervent appeals to their God of battles to bless each

their cause, which each had previously in the exercise
of their wise self-relying heads, stimulated more or less
by their passions, determined should be maintained and
defended by all the arts of war of which *modern Christian
civilization* can boast!

In another relation, one which concerns humanity perhaps more nearly than any other, inasmuch as every
child that is born into earth life is fashioned according
to its conditions, we mean the marriage relation, we
would ask, how nearly do men and women conform to
the true Christ life? Is this relation conducted in accordance with that Christ spirit which teaches them to love
one another as little children; and do they herein show
forth a living faith in those words of Jesus, " Whom God
hath joined, let no man put asunder"? The growing
tendency in all legislation to facilitate divorce, is a short
answer to the latter question; whilst the former is point-
edly met, by simply referring to the little improvement
in the human race, both in its physical and spiritual development, from generation to generation, notwithstand-
ing its changing conditions. But we have too much to
say upon this sacred topic, to enlarge upon it at this
time.

Other points of view might be taken, from which a
close scrutiny would show still further inconsistencies
between the teachings of the Master, and the lives of his
professed followers. Too long have these inconsistencies
been allowed to remain unmolested; too often have they
given opportunity to unbelieving critics to frame argu-

ments against Christianity, which no honest man can answer, and no sensitive soul hear without a blush of shame. They have been kept too much out of sight, and considered too much out of the reach of modern faith to remedy. But we hasten to meet the enquiry, which we feel is pressing upon us, " What has Modern Spiritualism to offer towards helping men out of these admitted inconsistencies "? We have been told, says the enquirer, from the Masters own lips, that the hardness of heart, which could not be touched by the sayings of Moses and the Prophets, would "not believe, though one rose from the dead "; and it can hardly be supposed that any less efficacy to convert sinners is to be found in the teachings of Jesus, than in the sayings of Moses and the Prophets. " Of what avail to Christians then, this modern necromancy " !

An enquiry based upon such a suggestion of argument, and it is the first suggested, the most natural, and the most potent argument that can be used, indicates the idea of Modern Spiritualism entertained by most unbelievers, and indeed by many believers, that the whole meaning and value of the phenomena is, in establishing the fact, that the spirits of the departed do exist in spheres more or less near to the earth life, and in the accompanying joy of communing directly with them. The truth however is, and we would proclaim it to the ends of the earth, to the many Spiritualists who are yet groping about in search for it, and to the unbelievers who stand outside hardly condescending to recognize the simplest facts of the phenomena, much less trying to ascertain their meaning, the truth is, and herein lies the answer to the enquiry so directly put, that these new conditions, and apparently strange relations between the spirit and earth life, are chiefly important as means to a great end, namely *the more complete opening of the heart of humanity to the influences of the Holy Spirit!* Thus, whilst we admit that the mere raising of the spirits of the dead is not itself of vital importance, however novel and interesting, and does not of itself possess any power to save, we say that the influences which the spirits of the departed, coming with the angels of God, are now empowered to bring and communicate to those in the earth life, constitute a new element of power not before manifested or exercised, at least in the manner, and to the extent, now permitted in this the fullness of time. The value of Modern Spiritualism is not to be found in those physical manifestations which strike so many minds as too trivial to be worthy of the higher spirit life, nor in those communications, which, though often full of beauty and wisdom, do not inculcate any new doctrines of life, or in their highest reaches suggest any better teachings than those already handed down to this genera- tion in the blessed words of Jesus. No, it is the in- fluence of the Holy Spirit, which filled the souls of the early Apostles, and is now waiting to be poured into our hearts through this channel of communication, this in- strumentality of God's appointment, that constitutes the real value, the momentous power and importance of

Modern Spiritualism. That these things do not originate
with man, most persons are now ready to admit. They
are indeed of and from God. Christ cometh that all
things may be fulfilled. Refuse not to believe because
the manner of his coming is not in accordance with
your expectations, or your human judgment of probabili-
ties. Remember how the Jews stumbled, because they
could not find in the humble Nazarene, those evidences of
an earthly kingdom which they had anticipated. Like a
thief in the night, is he coming; yet like a Prince of
Peace. Oh blessed light that shines through the dark
cloud which now hangs over this people, with a deepen-
ing gloom, unfathomable to the eye of reason. To the
eye of faith, the living faith as it is in Christ, which
can be known only through the heart, the silver lining of
the dark shroud is visible, and a divine hope awakened
to give new courage to suffering souls, which shall sustain
them to the end.

Modern Spiritualism is then no new "Cultus," but
rather a process in the development of an old "Cultus,"
amounting in its fullness to a new Dispensation. The
spirit world, with all its quickening influences for good
and for evil, is brought close to the earth life. The evil
influences come to tempt, to try, to judge, and be judged;
ministering spirits and angels come also, not in idle pas-
time, but in serious, earnest endeavor to reach the hearts
of those, who by inheritance, and their own contact with
the exterior world, are hardened against the things of the

spirit; and the labor has been, and is, to lift humanity into a condition receptive to the blessed influences which they have brought with them, even the influences of the Holy Spirit. Thus are all men to be raised up to a higher plane of spiritual vision, so that they can see and comprehend the meaning of the Scriptures, which are illuminated by this increased light. The truths in the teachings of Jesus are now vitalizing to the conception of believers. There is no longer occasion for scholastic criticism, or learned intellectual disputations, on the meanings of words; for the meaning intended to be conveyed by them, their true spiritual power and influence, flows out into the receptive soul independently of the mere dress, the external form of its expression. As in the days of their utterance, the words of Jesus were heard, but not understood; so in this latter day, their deep meaning, their full significance, their hidden power, their life-giving influence has not reached the individual hearts of the people, or never could the inconsistencies, and short-comings, be found in the modern Christian life to which we have referred. It is by opening the hearts of the men and women of this generation, so that having ears to hear, they may hear and comprehend, and carry out into practice, those very teachings of Jesus, that the revival of the ancient faith, the first great work of this new dispensation, is to be accomplished. Already has this work been begun with thousands of quiet Spiritualists, who are patiently waiting on the Lord; whilst the ever active and forth putting influences of Ante-Christ have endeavored to fasten upon the cause, the stigma of Bible Infidelity.

The power of this spirit influence is beginning to be made manifest in the development of knowledge of things spiritual, which is yet to be a wonder to the world. Only the germs of truth lie, more or less concealed, in the brief recorded teachings of Jesus. Germs of all truth they are, and first planted upon the earth sphere by him, through the grace of God, more than eighteen centuries ago. They have been all this while working their way through the crust of earth, their delicate points cleaving the hard-hearted soil in which they were set, and now, touched by the quickening rays of the returning Sun of righteousness, are beginning to send their branches out, and to spring forth to a growth, that shall be worthy of the long preparation. We are lost in contemplation of the possibilities of development in man's nature and surroundings, through his spiritual progression. These are, and will be, the natural growth of seeds already sown. They cannot pretend to be of any other, or higher origin than the early Christ germs; but in their development, there should be expected, in all phases of being, really new manifestations, new thoughts, a new understanding of the various works of creation, new conceptions of the earth life and its relations to the spirit world, which, as they spring forth, will arrange themselves, like new leaves in beautiful order, on the broad and ever spreading tree of knowledge.

We should be glad to explain our meaning more at length, but must content ourselves, for the present, with a brief reference to two exemplifications, from among the many which have come within our experience. The first of these, we find in a very beautiful and interesting manifestation of spirit presence and power, recently given in our presence, through a Medium, whose own spiritual condition is a sad evidence, amongst the many we have known, that physical manifestations have in themselves no saving grace, no healing power, but are only the necessary means of breaking down the obstacles which in this day of materialism, prevent the access, and impede the growth, of a living faith. After several other experimental tests, not particularly interesting to us, though calculated to astonish, and at least puzzle, a fresh enquirer into the phenomena; a piece of plain white card board, which had been carefully marked so as to identify it, was placed in the left hand of one of the company who sat next to the Medium. In the right hand of the same person were placed three pencils, two of crayon, colored red and green, and one of common black lead, so that they extended horizontally over the card board, and about two inches above it. The card board and pencils, in the position described, were then held by the same person under the table, out of sight; whilst the hands of all the others present were placed upon the table. Within half a minute, the card board was produced, and to the astonishment and delight of all, there appeared upon its before unsullied surface, a beautiful wreath, delicately drawn and colored, the vine and leaves in green, thick set with red roses in bud and full bloom, and within the wreath, finely written in black lead, but distinctly legible, a message of love signed by the name of a child, who was in the spirit world, unbeknown to the Medium, and to most of those present. Upon enquiry, it appeared, that the pencils had remained during their concealment, in the same position as first placed, a slight vibration in them only having been recognized. Our theory of the process was, that the picture was first conceived complete in its spirit form, then brought near to the card board and pencils, so that the elements of color could be abstracted from the pencils, and, as it were, photographed upon the card board by a power, of which we as yet know nothing beyond this suggestion of its existence. We could not resist the further reflection that in time to come, it may be long years yet, the relations of humanity to the spirit world might be so far changed and advanced, that this power could be brought into common practical use, in a way that would lift art to a pinnacle of power and beauty never before dreamed of.

Our other exemplification is not an external manifestation, but an internal unfolding. Through Modern Spiritualism we have arrived at an understanding of the origin, growth, and purpose of all earth life, of which we before had no conception. This understanding, like all our knowledge of things spiritual, apart from their phenomenal manifestations, is a natural out-growth in our

minds, stimulated into life by the influences with which
we were first brought into communion through the person, to whose deep religious nature, and spiritual development, we have before referred.* Little by little,
sometimes quite disconnectedly, with occasional direct
promptings, have these thoughts come to us, and by slow
degrees gathered to make a symmetrical, harmonious
philosophy of nature, which we feel is very truth, for it
is from God. Perhaps some of the ideas, possibly all of
them, for we are yet in our childhood, just beginning to
read the book of life, have been given to the world in
days gone by; but they come to us anew as inspiration,
for which we thank only the Giver of all good gifts.
Every growing thing on the earth plane has its spirit life
and form, and is but the external expression of the spirit
reality, the earthly habiliment of spirit life, made thus
external, in order to be cognizable to humanity. Let us
confine our observation to one phase of this external
expression; for instance, to vegetable life. We find then
that the office of the earth-born flower is, not merely to
delight the senses of man, and amuse his hours of idle-
ness or recreation, but more than all, to throw upon him
influences directly from the spirit life, of which it is the
medium of expression to his earthly sense. In form and
color suggestive of harmony, they accomplish much; but
as mediums for the transmission, sometimes of a life-
giving fragrance, and sometimes of a noxious poison, do

---

* Page 26.

the flowers of earth now appear to us as acting a most important part in the development of humanity. The odor is itself of spirit origin, and exists in spirit life, the flower being the naturally appointed agent, or me-. dium, to express it on the earth plane. Herein we find an explanation of what has heretofore been an inexplicable mystery to the best of science, namely, how the fragrance could be continually given forth, a real essence filling the air, and yet no discoverable reduction, or abstraction, of the substance of the flower. The skillful anatomist has dissected these little creatures of God's love down into their most inmost recesses, where the odor seems to have its birth-place; but the mystery is still unsolved, until we conceive the idea of fragrance existing first in the spirit life, and then poured through these delicate organisms of divine appointment, and made cognizable to human sense. The flower in fact gives nothing forth from itself, but is only the conduit, the beautiful medium for external expression of spirit life and power, and is able, be it never so tender and delicate, to continue its functions of transmission, whilst its natural life is prolonged.

Let us carry this conception a little further. Does it not throw a flood of light upon the mystery of human life? What are human beings, but the external expressions, upon the earth plane, of spirit forms and spirit life. What are we but mediums, all and each, in varying degrees, for the outward manifestation of good and evil influences, that are thrown into, and poured through us,

for the world's weal or woe! In one respect we differ
from the flower, and that is in the capability of our
natures, in great measure to determine for ourselves,
under the grace of God, whether we will continue to
be channels for the communication of much evil, mingled
with a little good, or whether we will become so purified,
through the life that is in Christ, that none but pure
influences shall be made manifest in our lives. The subject is capable of indefinite extension. We leave it here,
with the earnest prayer that all men may soon accept
its deep significance, and ever remember, that it lies
with each one to determine, whether he will draw from
his surroundings, and give forth in his life, poisonous
elements of evil; or whether he will spread far and wide
only such sweet, life-giving fragrance as the Father's
love vouchsafes to dispense through him unto his race.

But interesting, as we must admit such trains of thought
have been, and are to our minds, they are like all philoso-
phizing, insufficient food to satisfy those yearnings of the
spirit which reach up after the Father's love, as its only true
life. To drink from that fountain, "whose water shall be
in those who drink it, a well of water springing up unto
everlasting life," this should be the longing, as it is the
greatest joy of the soul. We welcome then those influences which will aid, as they have already aided many,
in finding that fountain of living waters, by opening the
heart and mind to a true reception and understanding
of the teachings of Jesus. And especially would we
remember, and try to comprehend the deep import of,

that saying of the Master, "He that rejecteth me and receiveth not my words, hath one that judgeth him, the Word that I have spoken, the same shall judge him in the last day." We feel, we know, that these words have a significant application to this day and hour. Christ, the Master, calls us to look into ourselves, and out of our own mouths to save, or to condemn. The Bridegroom cometh, we know not the day, nor the hour; but he cometh, and the angels are preparing the way. The evil that is in men must be eradicated, burned out from the face of the earth; and it will be done, nay is doing now; the elements are now gathering in for the final day, when God, through Christ, shall reign. As the lightning shineth from the East unto the West, so is the Christ influence now spreading, and spread, over the earth, quickening every good and evil element of life into new and unwonted activity. It is idle to attempt to fix any period according to our finite measure of time, when the culmination of these passing events shall be brought about. It may be many years yet: the processes of God's providence have ever been gradual in their development. We know not the day, nor the hour. We know, we can know, only the duties which each day and hour, as they come, bring with them; and this is enough, for it demands all our best energies to fulfil these duties with our whole heart. Under the Father's blessing, influences from the spirit world have now come to help us in their daily fulfilment, so that through a knowledge of God, we can say in very truth, in every

4

moment of each day, that we are doing His will; that His business is our business, and our business His; that our great desire is to be humbly worthy to receive the blessed salutation from the Master, "well done good and faithful servant." Thus, and thus only, will the selfish ends of life be lost sight of; thus, will men labor at their daily avocations, not to earn the means to gratify their selfish desires, but to do God service. Thus will they be practically seeking first the Kingdom of Heaven; and as surely as there is a living God, shall all necessary things, whether in their spiritual or material wants, be added unto them.

Let us then, each and all, thank God for the new Dispensation, whose work is only commenced when men, through its influences, begin to understand truly, and to carry into practice, the teachings of the Holy Book. In other ways of its own is it bringing, and will it bring men to the fountain of life, from which it is itself an out-pouring, the sweet savor of whose waters shall entice all who drink of it to follow the *living* stream up to its *living* head. Behold!—that "pure RIVER of WATER of LIFE, clear as chrystal, proceeding out of the throne of GOD, and of the LAMB. In the midst of the street of it, on either side of the river, *is* the TREE of LIFE:" * * * "And the leaves of the tree *are* for the healing of the NATIONS."

JANUARY, 1863.

www.ingramcontent.com/pod-product-compliance
Lightning Source LLC
Chambersburg PA
CBHW022149090426
42742CB00010B/1432